Bindings with Discords

Also by Pete Smith

20/20 Vision
Harm's Length
John's Book of Alleged Dances
cross of green hollow: elegies, allegiances, thefts
Strum of Unseen
Country the Colour of a Lithograph
Odden (I Sing)
Wanderlieder
Winterized: the Musical (with Hannah Naomi)

Pete Smith

Bindings with Discords

Shearsman Books

First published in the United Kingdom in 2015 by
Shearsman Books
50 Westons Hill Drive
Emersons Green
BRISTOL
BS16 7DF

Shearsman Books Ltd Registered Office
30–31 St. James Place, Mangotsfield, Bristol BS16 9JB
(this address not for correspondence)

www.shearsman.com

ISBN 978-1-84861-411-6

Contents

Part One: Pointes & Fingerings 9

One-Eye-Saw: "in the sure uncertain hope" 11

20/20 Vision 25

Evacuation Procedures 47

Part Two: Three Fancies in the Key of BC 71

Strum of Unseen 73

48 Out-Takes from the Deanna Ferguson Show 87

Mother Tongue: Father Silence 99

Acknowledgements 122

To Hilary
i/m Rhoda Smith, 1916–1994,
who never met a word she couldn't relish.

A Fancie [or Fantasy]

"When a musician taketh point at his pleasure and wresteth and turneth it as he list, making either much or little of it as shall seem best in his own conceit... And this kind [of music] will bear any allowances whatsoever except... leaving the key, which in fantasy may never be suffered. Other things you may use at your pleasure, as bindings with discords, quick motions, slow motions, proportions, and what you list."

Thomas Morley in
'A Plaine and Easie Introduction to Practicall Musicke', 1597.

Part One

Pointes & Fingerings

One-Eye-Saw:

"in the sure uncertain hope" *

[* misreading of a phrase in *The Order for the Burial of the Dead*]

The first person is singularly
ill-equipped for the tasks
the master sets & his hirelings'
endless computations wrap
an Omega round each riverring
Alph. A measure of inertia
dims everich briht sterre:
one-eye eclipse,
                    one-eye drop,
one on the blink –
romance's
            cleft.

*

Airs & Grace[notes]

for Lissa Wolsak

The banished me, the vanquished you
quickstep through slow sand of song:
the vanquished me, the banished you.
Dragged through the cerebellum backwards
flowering roots of syntax crumpled
phrase on hyperventilated phrase.
Score surrendered at the border
we who haunt the hinterland:
                              whistled air
          stopped holes   fingered
                                   graces

*

The name was cold:
wrapped itself counterclockwise in
          uncommon anonymity
& walked head-down into the blizzard.
A chinook erased the ice-shield,
resurrected braille ciphers.
     The feeling was cinerary, warmth
holding earnest
     of homecoming at harm's
          length.

*

Blue Muffle

Snow is aphasic
but its punctuation
immaculate.

So much difference
looking so much
the same.

Weight of white
suffocating:
cyanosis.

Snow's true profile lost
in the shadow
cast by snow.

Rumour of white
noised abroad:
fractal silence.

*

A Fine & Public Place

I.

In a heartbeat there'd be a block and a pass
and no escape. A heavy tackle could beckon
the sirens and weeks awarded with a nightgown
tied behind. Bed-rest ordered. Compliance to go.
Sign my chart and I'll don a straitened jacket, smile into
the mouth of an unsuspecting stooge. If all the world's
staged what's the rest but curtained silence, a hide
for a writer of headlines to project eponymous increase?
Prophet: a man who gains from loss. If it doesn't happen
in the margins, it doesn't. Surgical division: behaviour
modification by stealth: perseverations of dead air.

II Edengate

They say there's a level at which you'll find a playing field
where lovers dive over clover for cover.
There's no need for that, you say,
and there isn't. For an American declension, try:
I sue; you sue; he/she/it pays. We all pay
the piper and the cotton plugs that ease our passage
to the other side: no leaks and even fewer secrets.
Whether the Expulsion was strike or lock-out
is a debate hardly begun in earnest, yet,
in Texas, a branch was consumed in its own rhetoric.
Where there's fire there's someone smoking to get out
of there. Orbit or obit?
A nice discrimination: ash, dust.
Paradise downsized.

III Saul in the Details

The signal was perseverative: a flash card
in morose code – a depressive knows
a manic by his handshake.
You must have behaviour to meet
the criteria: what else is a *DSM* for?
His shrink is a rock wrapped in insight:
empathy is not now covered. Can we
call it MediCareless after the baboon's
heart disguised the baby's soul? Saul
in the mind: Paul in intent. *Swollen*
Members would have had a 12-inch
on their CV but the CD usurped them.
Is that hop, hip, rip, rap, or an oily film
Left by the incumbent? Gouge
the earth, O gouge the earth
and crawl thereon. Scrawled in crayon
on the belly of a 747
THIS SIDE OOPS: an act of treason
as to ruinate anagrams a leak
in the plumbing. As straight as that.
No straighter. No, straighter.
All chaste. When the lion pounced
the grenade blew Monday a hole
through Sunday. Raw roar; rank gong.
Inter mission: Burial Detail, fall in.

IV TIME'S NICK

Cradle a moment: it will lullay you
        into a false sense of curity,
make the chaos too tabular (wooden)
        to trust. When raising a truss
has ceased to be an act of faith as to wrap
        God in black leather quarto is to
contain nothing: the questions from whirlwind
        deserve better than to be answered.
Is and was are line-dance might-have-beens
        in-steps stepping out on the off-beat –
syncopation nation
        and a pay-back song from birthday brother
Marley. Flyers and catalogues
        and discarded ephemera will engage teams
of speculative researchers in reconstructing
        our times: a list of objects to conjure
the whit of a subject. "I'm just popping
        in 'ere for a quick one," he jerked
his head toward the *Mother Earth's Arms*.
        "Aye," she said, "'appen I'll join you later."

v Order of Dead
I am refuge to another.
Mountains seep past night.
Sleep-grass green & withered.
Angry days, years told.
Teach us to numb our days.
Wisdom us with glad comfort and prosper.

Now put down his feet.
Some body seed.
Image of earthly, image of heavenly, all change.
This mortal put-on: this sting of law.

The commitment of call-away.
The soul of ash.
This never-home.

*

Fisher of Men

"O, unreasonable salmon" (Bunting's Villon misheard)

As soon as he opens his mouth his mind escapes.
Tongue. Touched. Tinged with madness.
Not full immersion, a now-&-then sprinkling
Playing unreason – a fifty pound salmon
that, landed, would be a sinker.
Plankton memories: baptism by scale.
Leave your nets & follow him,
he may be worth saving.
An eyetooth for a lark:
a vinegar poultice
to carry blood a cross.

*

Say … All

Say someone steps in where there was no-one
where there is no in say this is not
cyberspace not a screened deflection of personality
say there was no chemical repression say you understood
the phrase *marital rubble* as used by Hejinian
why Snodgrass had his Hitler say
My failing was my kindness say you can rebuild
as fast as you can rebury the city is always tending downward no
matter how high you go say the phrases
of glass are shot through
with the colourlessness of dirt ground to sand say praise
is always in the mouth of the beholden say you wanted
to change channels in the middle of a conversation say
you did say no-one ever again wanted to colonize
another person say the Beothuk are living
in what innocence ever was
in an undiscoverable fold of the landscape say prime
rib clear cut hard knocks say the planet's
learning curve has plateaued say there's nothing
left say an astronaut came back
with something to say something shot through
with the colour colours come from say no-one could
see it say from where you sit
the word is indivisible an unqualified
seem of immeasurable wealth say the suture job was botched
and we are necrotic tissue congregated at the scar's edge say
the last time you used the word *word* you meant
world say the fast ball slides past your startled shoulder say the poet
is flensed through the lens of language becomes the scarecrow's
blind pupil at the sentence's close say nothing
closes until all

1996

*

A Little Skip Out of GMH (journal Feb 23 1872)

First glance: seeds of graves
stacked toward the east & the moon
just off the full
falling backward into its own
circus-ring of light; the grey sadness
lightened by bright blue bells in bloom.
A ghost of blue moonlight, second glance,
threads a fabric of layered clouds that calve
a fray of flakes & feathers from the selvage.
Refracted light brands the crowns of trees & shrubs
a nightgreen grey: the whole scene
in constant migration.
When March broke some ash fell,
leaving us less.

Evensong *[Coventry Cathedral]*

In this place, this slow mausoleum
space held by cold stone & glass
angles criss-cross
into shifting
open-occult wings.
Where sunlight strikes
air bleeds multi-coloured psalms
and when, in service, the choral voice
raises William Byrd, feathered
quavers trace the arcing roof,
fan
a rainbow of harmonic hope
then fall to ground, flame-tongued.
Profound expectations fibrillate
the hearts of the faithful. Some glimpse
doors in stone & burning air beyond; some
fixate on the eagle rooted
to the lectern's edge, freedom tethered
in its held wing,
law nailed
in its
claw.

*

Not All Trapped Things Are

for & after John Wieners

The metal mesh, windlashed & torn,
 leaks winged insects
the way a song from the Big O
seeds the airwaves with heartache.
For each one that gets in
a dozen hurl themselves uselessly
into the anti-mirage of glass.

Someone's always leaving.
Sooner. Later.

                                With the wings
of your cortex so burned
& torn
                who could stay?

A glitzy stanza; a man;
a night; an hour; an arrow-dented
amour; ten thumb-fumbled minutes...

All leavings...

Dum-dum-dum-dumdy-doo-wah...

The soul, though, do some souls
fly past the mortal nets

the fine powdered wings
carrying unbearable dumbstricken
beauty through metamorphic pain,
making the stone heart break...

so that the one I saw –
in a quiet peach space on my bathroom wall,
of the order Lepidoptera,
antennae alerted by the present danger;

his cathedral-window wings a partly-folded prayer-scroll;
blue hieroglyphs on grey parchment,
black limned – might have been a visitation
from this poet ("so fine/ this thing..., I am") –
                                        winged eye tiny enough
to weave, yes!, Blake's cosmos through.

20/20 Vision

"...words are one thing
reality is another thing
and between them is
No Thing..."
Jean-Luc Godard

Of sorts

Flags at half and pistols at twenty.
Beech-mast still pelts down.
The pace stretching our short days.
Evening out the stress bumps.
The tenor of morning an oratorio.
Another key where vibrato widens.
Spilt silt trickle spate estuary.
Semis, demis and demi-semis all a-quavering.
Just because there's a period doesn't mean an end.
The idea of body doesn't remove clothes.
Where there's a will there's a fisticuffs.
Way out west; way up north; weighed down.
A National Day of Morning: noon at midnight.
Mist of discharge fogs a dawn.
I half-doubt Thomas woud have rhymed that.
It's bigger than a frisbee, bigger than New York.
If a poem had enough combustion.
Eiderdown. Dander up. Relaxation always a middling.
The reflexologist said, "You remind me of myself."
The twentieth line presages an abyss, of sorts.

For granted

At the heart of every slogan a slip knot of words.
A sloppy knitted sweater of raw, wet wool. Made in.
The industrious revolutionaries plucked cotton from
the Manchester Canal. *Hey, hey, hey. Ya gotta believe.*
Scepticism makes the heart grow foundling.
There you go a sloganning. Wassail
will cure you: a week of sharing
and begging, a month of Sundays off.
Bread and cheer. A full belly makes a merry heart,
makes votes for the incumbent party.
The man said democracy will only really work
when everyone's got nothing. Crucify
that man, said the guard. The guardian
agreed. But I'm just a guest on this planet,
he pleaded. The tyrant said, Oh, alright
give him his own talkshow. There's a stone
to entomb a soul: the ratings always favour Barabbas.
When the judgement is suspended the hanged man curses
literalism. The word *promise* hobbles in on the crutches
of political sanctuary where not only the poor are taken in.

Back home

A home for the heart and the brain goes ga-ga.
Mushroom mush and rush of sixties nostalgia:
the poet is a creep in waif's clothing
and all her nouns are immortelles.
Tinkering with syntax requires a licensed
not an apprenticed: the little machine needs doctoring.
The ghost of a paper bag was not the first
collection from Birmingham but the first to see
in the *proper* accent with a properly tuned reality.
Say that word proper through a mouth full of blue candy floss.
Pockets of incense exploded all over the map
but the peace passed on, a drift of smoke,
an accumulation of regrets. The blue
turns into a Midlands grey: vowels overcast
in a deluge of consonants. Thunderheads
over the Fact Trees: chimney smoke
bleeding into clouds seeds the rain with acid.
The Midlands didn't invent the End of the World
but perfected it: grey foam flecks the Trent,
sun shines through a paper bag, sinks into the Power Plant.

About spades

When the wash is out it's not the same wash-out
as when the jig is up. If the wind is high
there'll be a new flap every few seconds
and, regardless of the direction of your intent,
gravity always wills you down.
When the English say, "Sod the Irish",
that's a literal spade of a sharper edge:
you (do you mind if I call you you?)
can taste the dirt, its dryness,
the dearth of rootage. *That bread should be*
quotes the lineage voice of Skibbereen
whose ancestors inherited the mass pit,
victims of the Irish famine, the English pest-
ilence. Silence in our history texts
another grave they're turfed into. Moon's thin
rib stuck to sky over Skibbereen makes a brooch
will not broach fullness – ever. If an image is still
permitted in this post-poetry: if the water,
pink-tinged, viscous, baptising the sink
washes away the sins of, the sins

Not yet

The summer of '68 we bought a budgerigar
but still couldn't balance our books.
The summer of '74 we fired our accountant,
cleaned out his cage and the lilac
waxed magnificent on his droppings.
It was the way the 0's failed to connect
hepped us to the concept of economic inertia.
We donated the perch to the Tate
after carefully removing it from the Large Glass,
preserving the dust in an envelope marked
Return To Sender. Phoenix, in the Arid Zone, a place
to park your trailer and await the Second
Coming. It was like a Vacation Bible School,
the Spirit was on *that* kind of holiday:
what rote and ritual failed to do, mind
expanding drugs claimed to do. Not every
claim is salted: we said *cool, wow, far out*:
the borders were certainly open, the guards all
chewed their tongues wondering how far that was.
The bottom line was a hook yet to be baited.

Off course

A large stumbling-block for man's mind:
a small spring in the heel of a mythical
healer. The gap in the wound neither skin
nor synthetic will cross. A gift of unknown herbs.
In the field of heart attacks the fox's
delicate gloves will box you back to health.
Brushed leather. Fibres abuzz with discharge
try to hold it. Hold it. Take the charge. Pass
it on. *A Book of Martyrs* is not a How
To Book; is not a How Not To Book.
Who veered this towards that subject?
I was content with the what before the how,
who wouldn't be? We seem to have lost the lead
from springer to cocker to blue heeler:
when the tail wags the poem you never know
what tyranny the content will be subjected to.
Between the teeth of the poem is a dangerous
place for an ego to loaf. Something gets ripped
out. He had to self-administer four sutures
because the skin was in a flap: heal well, humble flesh.

To oblivion

Daylight stole a march across open fields. Retreat.
From the front lawn lights of the city switch on.
Advancing into darkness, dimming and diminishing
the stars. Pretty words turn on an absence.
On the street small children skip rope, big others skip
school, go down to the park with the leather-clad
wankers whose delight is to take the sensitive, bright
boys in hand, teach them what no book can.
Class friction. Interrogation of the epiderm
by the epiderm: no answer. Any more questions?
All your adult life a quest. Not for a holy,
we'll settle for a nice one: a little ease
to tease the tired edges of our souls. Just another
commodity in a world burgeoning and burdened with things.
Even the poet shrunk to a witness. A tattered
kind of wisdom clings to the scarecrows:
crows gather on the elm and laugh into their wings.
A person sits sentencing words to oblivion, though knowing
better, sits at a west-facing window gathering dusk.
Outside a suburban brothel, mangled, rusted, one of Larkin's cycle clips.

No thing

The weight of equality. The deathward crawl.
State's cares. Love more than eye sight.
Image is a truth of the soul. Thee lady
and Albany's children perpetual. Love richer
than tongue? *Not born of comparison*
but of a reconciliation of two realities...
far apart. Opulent nothing. My heart, my bond.
The true blank of the eye. *An image*
is not strong because it is brutal or fantastic.
Right thoughts, just words. The price of daughters
falling: one's self and only dowry.
A resemblance of connections of a power. Scant worth
worth wanted. Kibes. Crab. Oyster. Snail. Horns.
For what is great is not the image but the emotion
it provokes. Village charity. Something, nothing.
Albion to Fliberdigibbet. A-cold and a-cold and no wind.
Born outside of all imitation and all resemblances.
The lashing of a whore. Apolitical office.
Heaven's crack, earth's glass misted with stain.
The deathward crawl. The weight of equality.

Home from

Roberto Rossellini said *all art now is always an expression of*
infantilism: suspect that, of course, dear reader, and, as your guide
through this random, subjective estate, I have to say such strident
language will not be admitted to this construction site. A high rise,
a low rider, a lower middle-class, high-density home away
from angst and mid-life crises. That's what we advertise.
A haven, you might say; two trees between which to sling
a hummock – no more outré fortune here nor a rose thorn-fleshed;
a cloud to hitch your dream to, that one you disintegrate with,
the one called *Gently*. Childish moaning, childish cruelty,
academic speculation on incommunicability, alienation. *Second*
Childhood the one-time harmless label: neurofibrillary tangle
in the hippocampus: the Maypole self a happy mass of coloured
ribbons with all the dancers gone. O dark, dark. *You do not die*
all at once. Some tissues live on for minutes, even hours...
a tissue of life in the body – poetical, political, personal:
there are outposts where clusters of cells yet shine. All go
into the dark. Outer and inner galaxies: no matter how bright
the transient flash, the greater mass consumes it. *Cruelty, infant-*
ilism, indulgence said Rossellini. *Attaboy* said God, *you're catching on.*

On fire

Yes, the Y chromosome is responsible for all that's wrong in the world:
anything that ejaculates is capable of total destruction,
every mother knows that. God was a lovely concept until
His trousers fell down: in Hebrew, in Greek, in public.
Some of the women will have none of it, others
sweat confessions through the pores of the confessional
until priests' groins flare in prayers of spontaneous combustion.
Joan of the Ark of this Covenant presides at the conflagration.
Her amour melts again in the sweetly,
saintly, sickly hyperadjectival postsynaptic sepulchre
of the Church of the Holy Kiss: the Betrayal
Kiss; the Kiss that Crucifies; the Kiss that Tortures
with Unanswerable Questions. The circumcision of the six-day old
member is not enough, a blink of pain to the nystagmus
of childbirth, the monthly stigmata of the blood:
the teeming unborn outnumber us, lurking in ducts, sacs, tubes,
they tell their endless parables. The man in the white coat says,
"Look at this: slits for eyes, tiny holes for nose, tube-hole
for the mouth the tube feeds. Look [2 inch lighter flame]: doesn't flinch.
Call that human?" Mitosis unravelled: shell of the unoccasioned.

But wait

It was a two-person coffin or a slot-machine –
you never know which in the crepuscule of consciousness.
Dim's the word when mum's been overtaxed:
the rest of the time there's no accounting.
So I said to this cherry on my right,
you may look bright and cheery now but wait
'til money's changed hands. It's O.K. to be
neon hope in the eyes of a starved multitude
but I'd draw the line at being government policy,
deficit haul. Still, a line of cherries is a change
of luck for someone: the same old luck for the one
before whose coin dropped into the general purse.
If you were to say, "What starved multitude?",
I'd have to say, "Money has no class but decrees by
deferred power: the many and the few don't even come into it."
I may find other ways of thinking, thanks to
the indwelling catheter or I.V. tube – the one
that giveth, the other that taketh away. Why not just let it
flow? Coin in: grab handle: pull. Three lemons,
three bells. Three of anything makes for a holy something.

If Not

If not a gamble a pre-rehearsed script:
if not a fated tableau a free-for-all where
neurobiology rules – O.K.? Whatever the big
picture, it's the little unexpected details that count
in my book. The Observer Book of Reckonings.
An Ordnance Survey Map of the Soul has been contracted
by the Central Government to the Anglican Church
the Archbishop announced today. A spokesperson
for the Ecumenical Watchdog Committee said there should
be enough folds in the landscape to hide a good-sized
non-conformist congregation as long as they meditate
in tongues and only clap during thunderstorms.
The name of that microbe that lives on a host in the sea,
comes out at night to feed and hides itself in its own light
emitted at the exact wavelength as moonlight slicing water:
that name for my pseudonym, please. Camouflage that pro
-tects it and its unknowing consort. Salvation on a scale.
What poet itching to be measured by what weight of salt
wouldn't want to be hidden, host or guest, by her words' light.
If not a poet a symbiotic marriage of wavelengths.

Within earshot

A poem that doesn't intend to entertain, that doesn't intend
to take off its shoes in anybody's home, that says
"Audience expectation? You must have the wrong show."
A poem that talks to itself all night long in a
language almost familiar but glamorously out of
focus: a poem that rests on the horizon with thunder-
heads gathering the force of lightning, the will
to move on the picturesque, domesticated farms
and flatten crops. A low, rumbling bass-note called soul.
In Henryk Górecki's *Miserere* wave upon wave of voices:
first the second basses then the second and first basses,
then the second and first basses and tenors,
then second and first basses, tenors and altos and on
until the whole massed choirs, with His name
Domine Deus, assault the tired ears of the Lord.
And having got, after 29 minutes, His attention
say, "Lord, have mercy on us." How tiresome for Him,
the constant petitioning: mercy, money, health, a clean slate.
Just once for someone to say, "I'm gonna give it to you
now let's duke it out." A David to whip Him with lament and psalm.

After kinds

Somebody's little girl: thigh-high boots and shorts, tank-
top, she invites, he said, the rampant prick, the paying guest.
Disgust of some kind is the engine, but we don't now if it's need
or greed fuels it. There's more than one way to skin.
One time he held an opinion then found out it was someone
else's so he lost interest in it. Another time someone said
"Oh my, that's an original," and he looked for hours
to see what was. He saw nothing, dimly wondered if
that was it, but deep thought's a foreign language to me;
more of a man for a pint of rough and a hand up
something moist and wriggly. As an act, she said,
of chivalry she grabbed the Sir Lancelot between his thighs
and rode it to a satisfactory. Two would have been better
but this was long before the discovery of the clitoris
while the Lady of the Lake was still fish from the waist
down. Evolution was a good concept for a wet Thursday
morning as rain pocked the pollen-gilded puddles;
but by Friday noon it seemed unlikely, the sun-baked
driveway wearing only dirty yellow necklaces;
to everything its whorl of stain, its mark and marker.

And so

There's been some ginger tom-foolery in the garden,
spraying screen-doors and trees, playing havoc with the dog's
nose. *It's that one from the other side of the creek.*
The evil from the other side, the ominous that awaits us there.
She had no sooner made up her mind than her mascara
ran. Decisiveness just brings us to the brink
quicker. Sometimes. Other times it takes us
nowhere: friendly Nowhere: peaceful Nowhere. Send your friends a
postcard from Sunny Nowhere. *Wish*
you were here. The decision to tame all the creatures
comes with a Biblical injunction: no higher authority
informs it. And so, sensing her true dominion,
she sent in words whose mission was to restructure
the molecules of his habits, but he fixed her
with his spellphone, put her on *call forward,*
call forward, call forward. Oh, boys, we leave
a trail of scent and, when we go missing,
the angels track us to where we've circled,
howling, the house of the last woman in heat. Full moon
gets the rap, but it's the testosterone cup runneth over.

Always only

D'ailleurs c'est toujours les autres qui meurent
but so few sporting the favourite tie
and the consummated smile. Toujours Eros
qui s'appelle Rose who runs at life, the trick to keep
the spectators from watching, reflecting
anything other than a ready-made rendez-vous
with the moment of the artist's perception:
his mating eye making all their moves ahead
for them. Something already made: the trick
to come at it again keeping only fore-
ground, whatever you can pack into one suitcase.
Play and making and the startlingly refound:
reframe that, hang that upside down, nail that
to the absence of meaning, sign it *That's life*,
the erotics of the mechanical, the stripped gears,
oil and mucus. He said, *Eroticism is the only ism*
to subscribe to. It's a given that if one body
is a hinge, the other's rooted to the spot. He would make a
voyeur of you, who said *live for whatever has no name.*
Cracked, the future will take care of the irony and dust.

How then?

First a shoeshine then the whole damned army.
Boot Camp to Boot Hill, they died with their
screen-savers on. When institutionalized non-compliance
is mistaken for revolution, it becomes time
to rewrite the history books: it always was
and will be. We brought our hands and mouths
to market when they said *need*, but clearly
they'd meant something else. Heroes cartooned
across the land carried by thought-bubbles
lighter-than-air and, sadly, poetics were not immune.
In the dream the Dismembering Conservatives Convention
assembled at Buffalo or Cambridge; accents played
each other like dying fish, and referents
littered the floor like used condoms. Some poets read
some poems. The empty hands at the marketplace were still
eloquent, in their gestures of disbelief eclipsing cynics'
tongues at every turn of wrist. The situation
explains the government: how then can anyone govern
in this Age of Image – the populace nesting, grouped
craws wide open screaming *Want Want Want?*

All over

Screen Goddesses usher in the era of the False Greece
to consciousness. Come-hithering and sashaying
their way they flick a serpent's tongue at pupils
and lo! stars in our eyes we buy the whole Empyrian.
The new Trojan Horse Channel brings in those outside
gods of misery, my Lords Greed and Mediocrity.
Come on down. Other technes create
instant nostalgia, break you and your dear ones
into timed fragments: zoom, smile, cut;
in your pram with soother, in your graduation
gown, in your senile frame with demented smile.
Misreading a sharp phrase in *the mode of failure* I get
razor charity: ask if it's hearts or minds governments
misread to have already implemented that? A little
soup, shaved bread, approved learning at the Consumers'
University whose motto reads: *A covenant with covetousness.*
The inheritance: atrophied left hemispheres and petrified
remote fingers. A legion would take up an awful lot of space
in your living room, but a lesion can be invisible for years
then erupt in a Vesuvius of emotional lava all over the rug.

See through

Another Night of the Living Idiot: Ritalin elasticated its Mick
Jagger lips in a high camp version of *Not Fade Away*,
extended by the evening caffeine balls-up. The wiring overload
kicked in in the supine position and tripped the rumination machine.
Daniel the Seer was so called not because of what he saw
but what he saw through. The statue's gold standard falling
to lead; the fire that doesn't burn you if you lick back when it licks
you. If it wasn't Daniel I saw with the Stones at the Locarno Ballroom,
Coventry, 1963, who was that singing *I'm gonna tell you how it's gonna be*
chug achugachug chug chug? Knowledge shall increase but still
won't keep up with ignorance: personal computers will refuse
to acknowledge your first name: the borders between city and country
will be patrolled by red-jacketed foxes. I, me, saw all these things
and was instructed to seal them up in a book to be published
in an edition of 150, under the imprint *Past Oral Histories*: *Six*
Six Six. The mark of a good beast is its ability to devour you while
maintaining eye contact and making you think it's worshipping
you. At the end of the thousand years it will be opened and read
and declared *Quite quite but John of Patmos has the staying power*.
Cities of gold; seas of glass; glitter that lasts, lasts.

For wards

The brain-washers met their Waterloo when it came to
coprolalia. The Battle of Tourette was fought on a
Yeovil playing field. Planned supremacy loses out to
random genetic interference every time: 21/23
translocation; a missing segment of chromosome 18.
The almost anencephalic boy is the barest encoded stem still
viable. We last saw him in his early teens in his cot
not flinching at the lighter flame held to his featureless face.
With his little-used name and the votive hope that guttered
at birth he flickers on, off in a memory loop. No Fellini
prop, he's in a ward north of London, circa 1969.
The Sigmund Freud Guest House is a run-down Gothic building
on Highway One that boasts a bizarre network of basement rooms
and corridors where signs read *Which way consciousness*?
Once poetry was a mole now it's all antenna, a raw nerve
flicked on by every shifting wave: reflection's for fuddy-duddies.
A two-inch flame: he didn't flinch; I did and do, who am his ward.
A man and his language being moved from the authorial plank
into the rough and smooth joins of prepositional demotic:
over there; to that; within him; against such; for us; for you; for them.

EVACUATION PROCEDURES

From the Ossuary

for Keston Sutherland

A broken may desire to move
          toward a healing
but the holistic is an arrogance
          immune to affect.
Songs were spaced along
          the lifeline, once.
They were married & buried
          together: the loning
has kept its primitive chord
          sculpture – pibroch
to the twelve bars of blue
          predictability: a soothing
& a saying to keep
          the unhale heartened:
a seventh leading back to
          home key. A dry dock
for leaky vessels, a scuttle
          of metal plates welded
by heat & rivet, "There, that'll hold."
          Water, sparing not a drop
of empathy despite its buoyancy,
          filled each lung & cabin,
corridor & trachea with its own
          unleavened weight.
A wreath of white lilies on ocean's
          disturbed surface hardly roots
grief to the spot any more than angst
          acts as rudder for anyone's
unconscious. Steerage is a class act
          to follow: depth measured
by ignorance's height above it.
          When the captain was unspliced
from the yardarm
          the tattoo on his ulna read
"If I'd've been a split stick,
          I'd have savioured everyone."

From a Priory

If the tongue is tied
    to the ear-drum
you'll miss all the rumours
but pick up repercussions:
    the shook & the rattled.

If the veil is rented
    out from top
to bottom you'll find salvation
's priced itself out of the market:
    indulgence going soft.

Cataracts occlude retinal travel,
    make statuesque shadows
out of refractory substance:
the infrastructure registers
    zero on the Richter.

The definition of disaster
    is under review
by the Insurance Brokers
of New Europa. Old bull
    on a 12-tone scale.

Perspicacity's a good glaze
    for earthenware
or brimming wine glass:
known to hearten, while a Curia
    is no remedy.

In a cave behind a veil
    the cataract
is tantamount to a cataleptic
rush of ululating matter:
    a failed Wasserman.

A Mantoux neither cures nor
        causes fluctuations
in consumption. Other forces
prevail, eg, the common wolf:
        the rest is palliative.

From the Dispensary

So, despite the moribund prospectus, he
put the asbestos from the dumpster in the landfill
& watched the redundancies climb to an all-time intractability.
Paradox is to poetics as coffin is to corpse: how
much light gets through is immaterial. The
boundaries finally break down: no consciousness is
an egregious estate with zen sheep pastoring themselves
while bullets graze the faces of Empire Loyalists in
the stands. The trick with tranquillizers is to have access
to & egress from the right neurotransmitter in the right
part of the circuit: when dopamine laps 5-hydroxytryptamine
it's time to call the dogs in. To inhibit reuptake is to flood
the market with good will: if more than a gesture
it becomes a lifestyle. The practice of mellow poetics
follows prolonged periods of mediation: rant relief
is a discipline will make amends. If it needs a fix
don't broker it. "Action potential" necessarily needs enhancement
if the populace is to buy into the industrial wisdom
of trading arousal for tranquillity,
that grand mediocrity.

From a Breviary

Shunday: excommunicants gather at the river, say it's pay-back time
for their redemption: a chaotic opacity in microscopic rewind:
good blood thrown after bad. *Maundy*'s prayers are full of carelessness:
its twists put idolators on hold: the random pattern – as before.
Chooseday's held over: a hymn to the never-ending sale: credit stretched
maximally: thinning on top. *When's-the-day*'s a lamentation: a silent
memorial for half-day closing: unaccounted time. *There's-a-day* without
wrath:
without mirth: unaffected: a flat-earth day: dissolution of monasteries:
enclosure of common lands. *pHriday*: service the shareholders:
neutralize
stocks' stains: launder the money: drown the people in acid: Selah.
Shatterday: kristallnacht: Shabbat in shards: the day Lucifer wrested
light from G-d: all this, he said, all you can see, demoting eye to a greed
reflex: immaculate foreclosure.

From the Plenary

First impression faint: blues licks on hot wax.
Where the tradition meets the cornfields; the crossroads in the kitchen.
A sense of meaning haunted the solo but bent it back into the walking
bass.
Those Mississippi breezes blew across the Serpentine.
More vibrato. Elgar swam upstream of all this
in the backwaters of the Severn; emptied Malvern's reflection
into the Bristol Channel, composing himself with every stroke.
Fording streams in our dry clothes we are spectators
at the Crucifixion, first hearers of the will, there for our title.
Music to be played on the heart's accord meanders through the Paradise
Garden: its arpeggios disperse us each with fragments of its fullness.
The Lord Lucifer, in attendance, dances off with the harmonics,
steels the thunder.

From a Binary

What rot god-wrought uswards
let noman put us under.
          Two for one for all for once:
          our muskets loaded,
                    ears cocked.

Plato's lovers sat impossibly
deflated in the Waiting Room,
          lorn, torn & ripped-off.
          Abby wasn't taking any more
                    referrals.

Neither-nor at arbitration
dropped the n=affinity
          to be absorbed by
          both-and: more dis-
                    than un-like.

Think of a number, think of
another, any number of numbers;
          think of a body trying to be
          one with all that
                    orbiting inside.

Clandestine trades brazenly:
the erotics of this exchange
          are charged at one full
          interest point above
                    the central bank's.

The value of metonymic stock is,
it's true, a Prynne derivative,
          but that market is not
          yet exhausted so follow the
                    ticker-tape trail.

The trick in figuring speech's figures
is to mind the thing & the likened:
    simulacrum & originary,
    the discrete demands
        of discretion.

From the Scullery

without oars rowing in the dark
stirring a storm in flat waters
the coxswain barks a rhythm to steer
through narrow needles & suchlike
metaphysical phenomena
a coracle to do the rounds in
a dream igniting memory cells
in their stored spiral washes you up
in the unlit room at the end of gran's
kitchen learning to discriminate
sweet pickles from strawberry jam
georgy bam georgy bam georgy bam
at three years improvised mantra
to the god of sweet things

RECESSES
TRADE WINDS
DEMOCRACY
HAYSTACKS
GROUND
CIRCUMNAVIGATE
CATHERINE WHEEL
SALVES
INNER SPACE
BONING UP
THE DARLING BUDS
FIRST HYMN
UMBILICAL LANGUAGE
ONE GOD AT A TIME

From a Capillary

Terminus of bloodstream last depot
            in a retrieval system
            subjected to weathers of which
the subject is barely aware: subterranean humour

Cyanotic alert a blue bracelet surrounds
            the wrist arouses faint pulse
            in heart's echo chamber
a cold front across the blood-brain barrier

Nutrient leakage is an elevator to wellness
            while floaters clog a body
            making it slow on the uptake
waste a total economy feeds itself ugly on

Eruptions boils pustules psoriasis volcanic
            ridges of overconsumption
            hypermarket shelves empty
themselves in a rush to the food bank

From the Olfactory

Licensed for pleasure
and versed in tradition
        in hendecasyllabic heaven
        he straddled the wall, inhaled
                on one side fruits in their season
                on the other burning flesh.

Swamped by irritants
air-borne and scoped
        he defended a weakened immune
        system, set about mopping up
                incontinent emotions,
                secured HQ in the lachrymal ducts.

Our creatures clover
and love long summer
        diesel scent clear than enough
        for jagged senses like in a river
                silence in grass and in black
                glare nerves our twisted words.

Versed in tradition
and licensed for pleasure
        she decants an entire eclogue
        quaffs a new winc, hcr old skin
                vibrant with unease. December
                hunkers down in its dank room.

From an Hallucinatory

Neuronal overload in Broca's Fold
a circuit shorted turning self-talk
        into a voice-over
        You say excite
                I say inhibit.

Overload? Overactivation in the left
superior temporal lobe. Better than what
        to have your shitty
        self-deprecation
                broadcast out loud?

A mute in a mafia overcoat
would have more fun at a
        funeral than I have
        weaving through this maze
                of tortuous wording.

An I traces back to source
following traceries of dropped speech
        ack-ack hauled from the edge
        hurled abuses defuse him (I) with
                chemical of their (our) choice.

Complexities become (increasingly)
undetermined: philosophers' shit
        becomes wisdom insufficient:
        fools' glitter: did you just snap
                me with your pen, fuckface?

The low drone soothes. The high squeal
is your (their) soul wanting out.
        The stone rolls back & forth
        in its groove: day, night, day
                & the damned, interminable words.

From the Refractory

Out of all hooping   skirting all borders
taking on all comers   flirting with totalities
for a second's fragment   they split
coffee break over dancing   singing
just a slob like one of us...
Policy didn't cover this & no safety
guidelines were broken though bent
was considered usual. One singer
doubled as manager which gave
forensic carte-blanche to the enterprise.
The convex mirror caved in as they rounded
the corner colliding with an obstacle
left there by last week's pessimist-
of-the-week. A stubbed toe was the damage
borne with equanimity & Tylenol. That *stranger*
on the bus was rumoured to have planted it,
"...the kind of thing he'd do", nods of assent;
"always trying to interrupt narrative", uproar
of approbation.
                                        The difficulty met melting
this back into the general schema was
taken as read. Rust-clogged bronchioles
clustered on the X-ray pin-pointing
fall in the Adirondacks. The Unusual
Incident Report stated you'd bc
hard-pressed to draw inferences from
this to assist in a future poetics:
"Theory is unusually anterior," it concluded.
Winter was coming but the pipes lagged behind
declining the fix.

From an Actuary

Under the rule of number
let us proceed.
Because 15% of men >50
develop prostate cancer

& that number is higher the lower
the income
we have no choice
but to place you at our
High Risk for non-repayment.
You qualify, in a word,
for our Eternal Bliss Life
Insurance coverage
but
the insurance premiums
so exceed the loan payments
plus interest it would not be
in your best interest.
Unless you
present your testicles
at this office by next
Monday 9 am sharp:
in which case we would
be willing to discuss a waiver.

Yours truly…

CHILDREN OF DIVINE
INDIFFERENCE

COUNTING

ON CHANCE

CHOICE AGAIN
DEMONSTRATES
POOR GRASP OF GRAMMAR

THE BUSINESS OF
PROTECTING
INTERESTS

THE BALL'S IN
YOUR COURT

SCISSORS CUT
PAPER

WHAT IS
TRULY YOURS

From the Chrismatory

Nine month living, six week dead: white shroud
laced with hoar-frost, trimmed with sod
its flounces swirl a vortex of singing, ring-a-rosy voices
sucked backwards over streets & fields to this
hole-in-the-ground.
                                        A policy in advance of a massacre:
a populace charmed by the smell of promised bread
on every table.
                              Oil of catachumens
                              oil of the sick
                              oil of chrism
                                        (olive oil & balsam)
                                                  to set a man apart.
Secured in a copper box, hid in a wall of the north nave
when superstition was to be uprooted, melted down.
Novum mandatum: on a Thursday, marching
orders, in the vulgar tongue, to get you to Friday:
one day, one time. Water floats word. Blood-washed.
Passed over & under-
mined.

From a Conservatory

Composer, given to dark fits:
process of elimination
even so 5-down was yielding
so slow there was no crop of letters yet:
fallow occurred but accrued
no takers in the horizontal field.
I'll try and relax
first try
then relax.
A forked twig, a sympathetic
nerve or two and there you have it,
another foundling poet dowsing for spirit
in the centuries' detritus: the piano
is asked to respond, does so softly
in sharp-scaled angles: the unhit keys
a cocoon of deep silence, a glaucous
spathe light seeps through to a frosted keyboard:
skeleton of a late German Romantic
moving in on the tone that played the surface
of his temporal lobe like a manic drummer
and effaced him cell by note by *agitato* rest.

From the Psaltery

If I were a witching you'd be quick
        enough to dowse that
        in all the magick
        water can muster.

Just enough to be clean on the outside
        & keep the blood buoyant
        on its roller-coaster ride
        ferrying food through to the flush.

Silt of ages, spilt for me
        cleave from a hide
        my thee. My vow of poverty
        had unhappy returns.

If you sign on the dotted swiss
        I'll give you back your willies:
        a chinook can kiss
        a williwaw still.

From a Lottery

The ghost of a chance slipped
            out of the starting-gate
& jockeyed for point position
            on the first turn.
The expression of air was manifestly
            the labour of the minute.
Up & over became a rallying cry:
            fences more aquatic than demotic.
A hierarchy quickly established itself
            among the fallen:
horses for courses, boys to the bar.

Meanwhile, before this interval lapses,
            home stretches out before you
in temporal fugue & largo.

Time is a narrow
            neck & neck   a chronic
opening. Leather on hide makes speed:
            hooves in air make myths.
A ticket to ride becomes normative:
            rogue numbers make a killing.

From the Presbytery

No rent on the god-house
though a bit ripped
when the tide turns.
The priest had to confess
his booth
was a hothouse for wankers
and oh dears.
She said
she'd see his Hail Mary
and raise him three carnal sins
for his indulgence.
                                        He accepted
the early retirement package
without the shares.
                                        Holy Orders
require sanctified compliance –
say do say do say do
down the hierarchy to our hero
the common man,
                                        who goes into
a room in the stone wall: the door closes.
Neither he nor his linen is seen
                                        In another zone
Mendl of Kotsk steps from his dark
study into the Shabbat-candled glow
expectant faces and says
                                        no blessing
                                        no promise
his silent Kaddish echoing
still

From an Ambulatory

You can lay it down
    but it won't stay fixed,
nail it to the church door
    and some upstart pope
    will remove or revoke it.

Late afternoon light
    pours, we say, through
the cloister-windows
    and washes, we also say,
    the millenia-old stone floor.

Light does none of that –
    the pouring, the washing –
by its own properties
    but through the innocent licence
    of a vision given tongue.

In such breezy corridors
    spirit takes flesh
on the expository tour:
    a guide is as good as
    a god – for the short walk.

From the Factory

The developers & realtors
are out for max prof
(no news there).
The shiny prospectus puts
– *Your Name Here* –
in the picture:
reclining in late Empire luxury,
up to your armpits
in bubbles,
you are the envy of your ultimate
self. The Bow River
Condo Complex
catches a lick of albino sunlight:
tissue-paper dreams
now flares
against a darkened future.
Shareholders get singed:
the insured,
cash-on-the-nailed, get lump
sums: what's subtracted
is the discrete
ingathered wealth of a lifetime's
travel & gift mementi,
each piece fleshed
by its own story. The underwriters do –
& the insured, post-facto,
don't – overdetermine
the value of coinage. No cornerstone can
save a fire-wracked frame:
only flame-language,
bloodred in its newness on ashen lips,
can build on the base exchange –
breath for breath.

Part Two

Three Fancies
In the Key
of BC

Strum of Unseen

[after Fred Douglas' book *Menu For Sunset: An Apparent Story Illustrated With Pictures* and his photo/text exhibition *Menu For Sunset.*]

"The lucky ones are the ones who can see the Emperor's clothes"

Fred Douglas

"They who had fed their childhood upon dreams,
The play-fellows of fancy, who had made
All powers of swiftness, subtilty, and strength
Their ministers...
they too, who, of gentle mood
Had watched all gentle motions...
Did now find helpers to their hearts' desire,
And stuff at hand, plastic as they could wish,
Were call'd upon to exercise their skill,
Not in Utopia...
But in the very world which is the world
Of all of us, – the place where, in the end,
We find our happiness, or not at all"

Wordsworth,
The Prelude, Book XI, from lines 125-144

Prelude

Gulls cawed to cling
            climbing the music

evoked jazz to execute
            an angular jump

An apparent healing
            engaged as smiling light

Pale music spiraled
            merged with ambient figures

Unlike the aliens their costumes hung
            innocent as a deer's anima

The aliens looked in awe
            at the memory of object-sculpture

First Movement

Once
for Malachi alone
something fluttered up
the hundred-year old stairs
green-gold-white light tall floating
his eyes still
shine with it the invitation
Unanchored story
seeks embodied memory
for a good
time
Redemptive parasite
seeks congenial host
experience an encumbrance

Sealed eye to eye to mystos
jutting
rock-cover decomposing lace of gullshit
cawed & cowed in caul & coil
surface calling surface
air-mail
splat with recomposed fish plasma

A focus of intense headway
an oracle scaled down
to a brass plaque of bourgeois motto

Feathers & puddled boats
float
force other objects from
the frame
the half-frames house other life-forms
a naked body on a bed
is a pink ocean of lip sink lace-work
while two
is a continent
of mis-fitting plates
a florid contusion

Burnished copper undercloud over Hyas-Pritchard Road
      & a redeemed copper plaque rising east
wind in aspens an aspiration of anxious reflex
      histrionic alright & at a pitch
                                                so they walk back
wrapped in only flames
                                    see nothing but feel
                                                            that licking
                  & the lack of the Great Grey Owl

A dazzle
lifts from darkness
      to metaphor you
this angel, so mechanical
you can smell the grease-job,
lurches across the gap
      but leaves you
                              undawned
                              stranded on the first shore
                              with no transport

Aimless wandering to quest as
uprooted alley plants to gardening.
no matter: fireweed & lupins,
swordfern & horsetails & morning
glories filled his patch of dirt
like crossword solutions,
                  giving it the air
dancing ceramics give kitchenscapes
or traffic mimics a dragonfly
remnant choir

                  All-night café's
OPEN's
      green-orange glare
                  tells a story
that blooms into borders of
      loosestrife & forget-me-nots
(& anemone that choked the poppies)

its path wanders in & out reality
past the disconcertingly familiar enemy
    & the dancing, waving dead
through delicate maneuvers with fixed grin & bayonet
to discharge itself in glorious ambivalence
    in the white margin's maw

Second Movement

M Bob is delighted to learn
both his middle & his mum's names
are palindromes
                    See, we go out
                    & we come back in again
Sometimes
from the way he's looking I'd swear
he's living both here
                            & elsewhen
bellows   concertinas   spirals   lungs

        Saxophone swannecking
            through a cigarette-smoke curtain
            sun's high beam
                dimmed by maroon & ivory drapes
            filters the heroin/e
                cracked voice
        The 1950s stainless kitchen
            is a steal – chrome on linoleum
            makes the grilled-cheese sweat gaudier
            prepares for the photos developed in grease
                an apparent rose
                baby's face the blue-red of a blister
        through a thin fog
                ...until then I'm trav'lin' light...

        Mother climbs the wall with
            the baby's wails
        its liquid wishes a fish
            out of oxygen
        its needs
            a slap of kelp

        At the Indoor-Outdoor Café
        someone's scratched
            escape-maps
            on the wallpaper

She looks anorexic but may just
      be biding her time
      cosy to comatose is
            a short trip off the couch
      if the TV's too big
            for the room
            you're just
another deer caught in the headlights

Sights
            dim
                        strength
Cult adam avers my father's thunder
The hard fall
like candle waste
                        wax proud
at the last joy
to light up posthumous
                                                word.

LIFE exhausted him
      not the content, the layout
      the self-inflated running
      commentary
                              captions
      shrink-wrapping each experience
      Currents & Events & Awards
      all shined up with Brasso
      culture-plaqued
                           the trivia
      gather in a sepia car-grave
      its yawn a perfect catch
                                                      all

Lute Solo

out of the blue
        the other blue
a flotilla of crafts
        sewing new skin
on old bone myths
        a potlatch exchange
not outlawed but alien
        not many but one
many-roomed mansion
        hovering overhead
you begin to taste the liquid
        charm of their voices
reel at the harmony of
        their vision – just
in reach   a small leap
        & you're on board
The Golden Age yet half-
        remembered word stirs
trouble as you're pitched
        from shadow to shadow
the golden age we look back on
    and the one that'll be sifted...

Third Movement

Malachi Bob
has dropped in here
& rederanged the set
The van
is now upside down
with the deer atop its bottom.
A half-coloured velvet
Spiderman drops & drapes
over the lot
(given him by a man whose medical history
tells he used to be associated
with the Hell's Angles).
From
all geometricians of darkness,
Spiderman, preserve us.

Self-portrait of feet
glowing gold & white in
the paradise van,
I mean, the camperized van
everything fit & ship-shape
while you're enjoying elsewhere
she applies for a position vacant
you're hardly aware of advertizing
performance poet, beat poet,
person poet, post-conceptual-
modernist-languoring poet,
poet-in-residence-at-the-navel-of-the-world

She turns out to be Martha Stewart's
Hungarian cousin & is a dab-hand
with caraway & paprika
their days are a medley
a smorgasbord of peasant
& haute (easy on the haute)
a tart parsley wine with the
sauerkraut soup

An analgesic traces the route
from purse to nails to lips to tongue
undulates down her pink throat
to wait in her stomach
for dissolution
passes through all the colours of sex

one: desire & music are a vortex
two: the rhythm the rhythm the rhythm
the rhythm *three*: dithyrambic
celebration collapse
bottom fish sit this one out
on top of the news
four: slow dance among the picnic debris
lives measured out in steps
portraits of soles on the move
    & at rest
waltzing through wilted lettuce
    crusts of cheese
    crumbed stones of bread
dancing away from stilled life

Stories of an untoppable utopia
lend a certain ambience
to the manufacture of toilet-paper & flints
    a fright of half-chickens
    runs around the compound
    like a political campaign
    giving birth to votes

Tintinnabulation of their voices
    carries their presence away into
    the crepuscule erasing the far trees
On falling silent
    they come into themselves
ringing tones   disappearance   return
& content obeys those same tidal laws
    the words all make vivid sense
        resisting meaning

Fourth Movement

Every shrine opens onto
with a cross light curves around
but never penetrates unless
a wall is a wall until a door
down the sudden staircase step
two figures bejewelled
with lovely household gadgets
Mac's drawing is of a short
tall van with seven doors
It's for seven very tall skinny people
He is pleased for the seven people
and the driver that they have
such a van
and that they will always be
this happy

All the stories they'd ever heard
were now a Swiss Cheese of the fifth
dimension amended by refusals
silences & long non-sequiturs
threading
over the corpus callosum
dendrites of missing
narrative staggered
like victims of mustard-gas
while imaged roadblocks
stirred up a paralyzing nausea of nostalgia
at the Café Biologique
the procreation menu was off –
the chef away on a libidinal hunt

It could be lizard pie à-la-mode
served with jello
& a kiss of killdeer
it's a scarlet soup with indigo streaks
& a yellow animal
that blesses you

while sacrificing itself
on your tongue
it's a taste of family
with guest & host run through
the blender

In the window seat of the lounge
inner & outer space track each other
parallel nowheres
interior decor can be the place
indecorous memories spray
a little kitsch in your soul

There's empty lingerie lined up neatly
where our women used to be
segued seamlessly into
It doesn't matter 'bout the weather –
we'll steal the old folks blind
with two penny-whistles accompanying
it into *Saw myself on the street*
last night – a lot of stagnant waters
she's bridged & a raucous rendition of
It's the biggest postal district
in the world with a sudden chorus-line
stamping & licking in perfect sync
echoed laughter crashed
into unminded fragments

Too much flow
in a farrago of genres
too much undertow
in a torrent of stasis
(Haptic reader
we hope soon to raise you
from the mire.)
When the only light in the world
is coming from without
you know you'll never find
the handle.

Cor Anglais Solo

No go

    the twist-tight root

April glut

    rainbow weal

Aching mouth

    holy tongue

all sad and cloud-hung

Coda

As if in post-coital tristesse
overcome by the sense of empty perfection
that had briefly baptized them
            our she & he
leap off glance up to see
the nose of a prop-plane
like the nose of a stoat
propped
on a fetish of snakeskins

Giggling with relief they agree
            here is exotic
enough & watch the sun set
on Malcolm Island
as the Finnish-Canadian
women of Sointula
saunter home
in twos & threes
sunlight flashing
an unreadable code
from their fishbone
chokers

48 Out-Takes From The Deanna Ferguson Show*

"*Unlimited growth increases the divide*"

*This work arises from trawling through DF's poems & from brief encounters with her & some locations in Cranbrook & East Vancouver.

1.
There is failure of community in the poem-world of Deanna Ferguson. Reader & Writer look like Sisters, even Jesus would bride, while religious ecstatics around him soil their habits & mortgage their futures in a TGTBT Ponzi scheme of vertical assent. What goes up must... etc

2.
Causal defects tell us teaching gets in the way of something & maybe it's something you've read. Some *place* meant *situate*; some *hold on to your tilt.*
The poem teeters on the edge of the 32nd floor. Its own yells of *Jump* outshout the crowd of eager enablers.

3.
Let me introduce you to my anthology. Your absence will guarantee you pride of place.

4.
If *confuse* is a privilege *refuse* is joy unbound. Drain & squirt & mercy me the holy of holies defuses the Prime Minister's larynx. Speech! Speech!

6.
Water or Knife. The real cold shoulder doesn't discriminate edge from edge. Precipice shower: prospect point.

7.
Link fantasy to *Lulu*, inexplicably: sing the syntax 'til the bell claps out.

8.
Cranbrook – a long hop from Kent to this mountained place where unpoliced theories home, eg, *mental conceptions*, *hockey-dad* & *gourmet logging-camp chef*. Wait a wee minute: just cuz he's a drool case, there's no need to get peevy.

9.
If you hit Louis Zukofsky twice with a 2x4 you'll get a demi-semi-quaver discount of Coltrane or a Sophie's Cosmic refund at 4th & Arbutus. Not both. Not likely.
A word in your (ear). The poem as high chthonic lavage or syringe me an aura, Poe, peel me a bell. Both. And. Trinkle tinkle.

10.
Shut the window. The stench of bad poetry is affecting my equilibrium. A pocketful of posers is no help.

11.
Fear is Gaelic for *man*. Fear goes on. US policy: them murderous unbelievers. The domestic, the foreign, subjected & objected to.

12.
The thought of an audience, that's scary.

13.
You can read my *Writing*, Tom.
Yeah, then I can stand beside my text, be a para/graph.

14.
Blazoned on the Ferguson clan heraldic crest, a heart with a nail through it. So bleed, language.

15.
The thought of a reader, that's too scary.

16.
It is true that Oprah refused to appear on *The Deanna Ferguson Show*
& then she declined.

17.
At the AmLit/CanLit border the guards have dropped theirs. Keys. Lids. Hastings deserted: Hamilton abandoned. Acid Speed Toxi City.

18.
D. Ferguson & T. Raworth read *together* at the KSW. Not together, she first. Her words so angry she whispered them & we groped round in that lacerated silence; his so fast we lashed ourselves onto the raft of her silence & went over the falls together.

19.
Ground swell   water OK   air fair
-to-middling.
Lines in the sand for those who cannot read
the signs in the land.
The waste. Not whatnot.
If oysters turn sand into peep-holes
then Tom's a-cold, but a dry cold.

20.
Someone was watching, always is, while hair & common standards fell. Tom, Hugh Hefner's little page-boy, who saw him peep? Godiva didn't. Her collective eye was on the way her smooth hair swayed with the horse's wind-roughed mane: the illusory politics of freedom. Leofric breathed a corporate sigh.

21.
Hello you little Bombshell. I was just thimking plastic explosives need a lot of room to grow in: neglect of poverty to acidify the soil. The rich have problems too: first, vertical running water at False Creek, then a high-priced flotilla weeping all the way to the bank-on-it.

22.
She daughtered well, but there was a huge draft when she quit her post
at the lacuna between door & stoop.
Muck thirst ensued & matching of teeth.

23.
Carrying on down the line. Lots of fuss over Onan's under-determination. He wasn't such a bad wanker: interruptus was the issue. Refusing to co-sire through his dead brother's widow. Not following the line of morbidity. Patriarchy required such hankies.

24.
She lives way up there. Doesn't connect with the Collectif any more.
Disowns her (previous) poetry.
Does it still speak to/for her? Six/eight then?
Even as time's signature shifts the relative minor may still bring gladly home.

25.
I say/cannot say: indignant is as disgust does.
Gust of foul wind
hard gist
expelled guest
aghast
sex-ghost
gloss this.

Inertia caves in: woe beside you.
Pride out-sources itself then trips over its sorcery.
Dr. Susan Miller says disgust is the gatekeeper human
emotion.
Protohumans: the disgusting or disgusted?

26.
The putative stars of *The Little Coup That Could* accepted a time-shared condo in the North of Contention in exchange for revolutionary fervour. Proof: every reaction produces an unequal and opposite inaction. Don Carlos Williams produced Don Paterson out of inert matter – a three-step program where twelve were needed. Being one of the boys is the apotheosis, but notice how quality control always rises to the top of the boot.

27.
Sometimes the subordinate is to keep in place: it's skip-rope without the count. In group therapy the *maladaptive* follows a dose of strong *socio-chemical intervention.* Evolution drags such nets.
In opera if you lose the key six degrees of grin & tonic will see you home. In both, sign by sign, the show must go

28.
To Elvis. What the US Army needs in Iraq is to Elvis:
have benign capitalist pill-poppers show how easy
the Good Life is for all
in a non-prophet society.

29.
Love-lies-bleeding. Inca Wheat. Pigweed. Tumbleweed. Amaranths.
Amen.

30.
A river runs out of it
            keeps girls & co-eds tamed
                        clouds the fact
that Hero was a woman
            fell
                        for that drowning boy betide

31.
Disarmingly, the tree was perchless for the bird.
Chopped & lopped & follies ahoy.

32.
Or not to Elvis. Splick, splack I was taken aback.
                                    Hard rock, hard island,
                                                Hard line
            Eye to eye looking   like want wants want.

33.
          Swayed & stormed
He wishes for us, from the City of Men,
          a health of ripe waters.
Hero was still woman
          also the Beloved.

34.
Everyday dust say You rather be a poet or write poetry?
Just dessert is more than I can afford.
Alice, be tactless.
Nevermore than an extension of Raven.

35.
Silence then. An honourable estate. After all there are already so many more poets than poems in the world.
                    Unsay. Unsing. Steel home.

36.
Half of me thinks stand-up comics should stand in buckets of their own piss and half of me thinks a sentence is a pustule of fascist pus while half of me idles in neutral and dreams of fifth and a ten K passing lane in the always-up- ahead…

37.
Political heartsickness for *asphyxia.*
Don't you wanna choke on that?
          Hot bush   Singefingers
          Preresuscitated angel spirochete
          President of an abject state
Katydid or would have if Remorse hadn't winged by.

"We will find Original Sin whatever rock he's hiding under: we got him on the run..."

38.
How do you turn your back on yourself?
        When the learning-curve turns into a cul-de-sac
                there's no stopping progress – is there?

39.
The story goes round and round:
an intimacy shared is a braille invitation – unopened.
        The ubiquity of bullshit makes detection difficult:
        the chosen forget the choosers by nightfall – apparently.
                Until representations   no fear.
Depression loves a warm gun: happiness prefers cold cuts.

40.
A yawn of clomipramine.
The atomic part tickles –
                fields where late the sweet burns

41.
Hush, what erotic breezes drift over the marsh.
The subsequent renga to be published by Sudden Change Press.
No matter how softly, vengeance is a mine of hideous non sequiturs.

42.
He thought you could only use a Swipe Card if it was stolen. Like a urinal with no brain-pan.
Back at the shop when the spleen was removed the poem was nothing but cut fist.

43.
The stand-in person eschewed blotting paper
spat out wasp-sting.
Hey, you, mean it like you act it
nerve-pulped
& easy on the butter.
A rougher prejudice writes without dallying
the bluest fade

44.
Tinge me an orifice, won't ya.
Hang & clang
until the rats say it wasn't so
total eclipse.

Odious & Amorous sat in a tree, mewled & wailed,
bade the owl burrow
& singe some artifice; some holy.

45.
They told us a little economic SSRI would fix our Recession, so we borrowed it from the future. Not ours. Some other losers'.

46.
It's the Law of the Biggest Dipper, the one whose ante is so far up everyone & her philosopher folds. A silent bid on eBay will at least raise an old hope for new heaven & a private government will clean up here, in our time on our dollar. There is no way. Out.

47.
She's uptown now
Is that a place
Has it a poetics
An eco
no mics
(no scots either
Is it refuge
assault
high rise
irony
low
lands
away

48.
Those are words that were her poems
(chiastic chasm)
When you amputate your poem-self
do its nerves still twitch
in the night   at lunch at sex
in mid-conversation
that phantom limb
& its gathering brood

Och, her imagined voice says,
pull the other one –
tintinnambulate yr crippled
poems outa here.

Mother Tongue:

Father Silence

1.
Within the frame Spencer had always had that *flair* for painting the roundness that everywhere cushioned his erotics. Even in the Resurrection at Cookham Churchyard the dead would *slip* their grave-flesh and make carnival – overflowing & puddling into their incorruptible flesh – *tongue* to breast to bountiful thigh. His tumescent brush chased & caught this: chaste & cored. That dance.

lair slipt tongue

2.

When a glove *dream*s of hands it is not moved by loss any more than is a believer-turned-sceptic: the sun rises and sets on glove, dream, love and ream. No-one/thing redeems every-thing/one. As stones into wall, threads into glove, bone into bone are *knit* so earth weaves its guests into that time-warp – ground into ground, ground above ground, ground beneath zero. Awakening glove puts on sanctified airs: work-gloves wear dirt with pride. We all unravel down to simplicity's *genitalia* and further down to first lust.

dream knit genitalia

3.

Whirled and whisked out of place wearing their melatonin brand the yellow peril pickt up in *swirling* xenophobia is dropt off the edge of the map. *Aureole* tracers haunt prairie horizon. Up root and trance plant: soil is soul's home after all. Where the wind puts you, where the whim, where the whin... Eye takes it all in small measures: the vastness one pixel at a time. Pixellated and transfixed in a transept eye follows a shimmering that you walk into. *Chapel* of ripe corn yellowing in feral serenity.

swirling Aureole Chapel

4.

Bamboo-heart, water-heart teach us the meanings of friendship. Between heaven and earth, a journey to share – everyday home. Be with until public *law* – BC Security Commission, March 4 1942 – states you are decreed nisei, sundered by stained *metal* blade of fear-hatred-greed. “Relocatable persons” are asked to be rootless, artless, homeless &, best self, lifeless. Everyday home *clap*s you into its pure bamboo, empty water jail. Be your own best friend – a shade yellow, simulacrum/b of white (boss) man – bereft of former chums.

claw metal clap

5.
Unharried… the old year sucks up the scold. Year's end, year sends a new one in its place. Cicada's sound at Ryushaku Temple, May 1689, resounds in stone on Opal farmland, 1942. *Lattice*s-of-summer's ascent a scented air of psalmic blues where *fluted* iris lift funereal heads, where beheaded tulips leave lanceolated leaves to spike the air with *grief.* In Izumo Oyashiro the Ancient Tree sings its long-, its short-lined rounds tessellated with paper-prayers that would telescope into the moment all that it can hold.

Lattice fluted grief

6.
At Emma Lake titanium white makes a new man. Hoarfrost patterns hexagons on broken ground of reds & *dormant* blues – quick strokes of slow song. What is refused or repudiated... what remains outside... persists as defining, as founded and continually refounded, as spiral *fountain* of unleaving. Finding himself dumbfounded and double his subject residua play *host* to cohort moths inside a tall well of light.

dormant fountain host

7.
Stop the mind. A stop the mind makes. An image is a stop the mind makes between uncertainties. Sure? Sure. But, he said, if she draws it out of you it's an elemental commotion. He almost said. An entrancement to *clasp t*his eye to that space. Opens to draw you in: that's her point in space. If you don't get it the mark's pointer remains *unseen.* A curving abandonment: a signed exile deep in the page: self recovered, found in being-looked-at. All rise. *Palimpsest*: Kipling's passion for entrances; Spencer's for emergence; Kiyooka notes both, is the brassy smith of such rubbings.

claspt unseen Palimpsest

8.

Whoa there, white boy, who you trying to colonize now? What you up to, dry-humping Kiyooka's spirit for a poem for your trophy wall? Wearing that retro-compassion on your sleeve like an old bandage with its rising sun of blood? Who you – some *Rimbaud* of the suburbs sporting your flaming green hair into the nearest Starbucks? Just 'cos your Jesus *wept* all the way to Golgotha doesn't make your tongue clean. Back to your drawing-room, check that old atlas tessellated with red wounds. What the nothing you say? There's many kinds of *silences*, yours is just a hidey-hole. I never saw the white oppressor in myself until i… There you go again! Yes. I do. Go. There. Oh, yeah?

Rimbaud wept silences

9.

oh let the semen fall where it may off any horizontal field green-grass growing chokeweed empty sky reflecting a cracked measure of a people taking dominion seriously to the ends of the earth *dangling* participles of a subversive people scrawling scrolling down-page in upstart nerve. *Dreams* rice-paper frail talk utterly other syntax. Pigeons on a rice-peck scurry against a backdrop of dark yellow fields of mustard. Forgive this offense please, am present here only to return *unspent* portion of heritage: language taxed with neglect of

dangling Dreams unspent

10.
The privileged discourse silences the needed discourse: freedom (of speeched imaginings) trumps slavery (known & lived) every time. Takes its *breath* away. What gives? Give is to offer as altar to petal, vision to leaf – let the least thing (grounded or aired)'s least gesture grasp your *tongues*, eyes, ears, yesses. Offer petal & leaf to the god-of-this-world: not to appease him, but to focus you. Your wording. *Quarry,* he's a no-name Jap haiku blues singer: explorer, his tongue mines Indo-European rooted West Coast Canadian easy-talk. Beat or bereft, he keeps coming up for more aires.

breath tongues Quarry

11.
Take the tongue, flaps & all, tie it in nots. A tongue held, within a written sentence, blisters. A father's held tongue swelled & blistered in the son's mind: a mutual silence a*rose* – thorns wrapped in silk. Father Silence can be tongue-tied refusal, thick & opaque, or *burnisht* wisdom: Shozo (12), trousers; Minako, school-badge, name burnt out; Akio (13), school uniform; Takao (14), leather belt; Miyoko (15), one clog… that harrowing, those bequests, reel him out of the Museum, and later – "nobody can live inside the Monstrous very long without becoming one", father said. *Wing* of next world, spliced frenum, hinged here…

rose burnisht Wing

12.
Now that the Collected (out-of-print) Roy Kiyooka the non-existent collected prints of Roy K Kiyooka the uncollected existence of the Princeroy Kiyooka that Roy Kenzie Kiyooka *still*-proud grandson of Master Masaji Oe has lived out his democracy of attention – yr story yr acts yr presence honoured in his yet-*undreamt* utopia – his cleft tongue singing cleft prints marking a place athwart the United Static of Centralia alived with Kiyooka-being *stirring* still abandoned in words in curves given over to re(dis)covery now

still undreamt stirring

13.
Complicity is a dance. Solo or national, it's a line-dance. Recruits its verbal firing squads in kindergarten. Hold that line. Toe that toe. A shadow dance. *Night's* empire holds a white flag to a red bull. No charge for that. Back in '83 My Union Jack patched the seat of My Levis. The western day will have its dog: in purple descent through *labial* air, not less were we our alien selves – a hidden ancestral muscle pulls this writing tongue. Speech is where I's at: and there, I'm all over the map. Hedged in by hegemony, language is the first tyrant (victim) of war. Complicity is an eschatological dance – coinsured, you put your whole selfs in. Share this. *Dividends* paid at term. Smooth-tongues always keep the turkey in its pen. So oppressive, the dog days of empire; the white-outs, tongues erased…

Night's labial Dividends

14.
Unmasked. Bare-handed, fathers & sons dig pitch-blende from mother earth. Pins on a corporate map flag its route, Deline to Los Alamos; on a military map, New Mexico to the West Pacific. From Dene soil to air above far land of *an other*-tongued people. Critical mass: pivotal cupola. From a two thousand foot tall pulpit, Little Boy preaches a *radiant* gospel; converts masses. A baptism of wind, a thousand miles an hour, hurls thousands out of themselves. *Gutter*ing air & flesh, tongues of fire dance maniacally across a rubble plain. From the margins of Great Bear Lake to the epic centre of hell, Dene elders bring dignified apologies, who didn't know pitchblende's yield, had no way to imagine the elemental yield of uranium 235. Eldorado mined & refined: Hiroshima buried. Resume masque.

another radiant Gutter

15.
The past not uncommonly takes a while to happen—*clasping* that little nugget the question rides its 50-year wave of silence: O where is the Adorno of Hiroshima? Has she spoken yet spoken yet spoken – ballooned words into Amerika's *parenthetical* guilt: that oxymoron. The crime of that Yank-Jap, Yasusada, was to stir memory? Beaten to a *pulp* by righteous editors he erupts as mid-Pacific atoll, as tsunami rolling to wipe out his presumed birth-nation's amnesia. The suck of such false tides betide us.

clasping parenthetical guilt

16.

Exiled within exile. In the county of Thorhild, Opal, Al: eight futures on the altar of the god of war – we put a little yellow in the opalescence. In a log house with sod roof – no electricity, toilets, water, *snow*ed in for months. Moths beating against our genetic flame. Farmers from Ukraine teach us the soil's ways – hard but workable – include us in their barn-raisings, their birth-to-burial rounds. Here, far from Anglo-Canada's *bloated* sense of niceness, a shine of fellowship. Life comes at you, at a trickle or a fast scald, take it; weave into it the lively & the sordid. From the bustle of Calgary market to bleak Opal earth: *root* sellers to root-cellar. This Canadian heart tires & numbs while my Tosa heart pulses its deep song.

snow bloated roots

17.
Everything has its time & its only time – Heraclitean so you cannot step into/out of it. At exactly 12.30 a.m. May 18th a much beloved pear-tree was toppled by repeated gusts of alacritous wind & its crown visited the *astonished* lawn. Poet & poet watched from bedroom windows & cradled their *breath.* Pied pair, pith, stem, seed grew into one pote's book-lament: one embraced absence. What a lovely hardwood fact that the pear-tree *call*ed to be by Kiyooka's ink-breath will outast its source. Ah! that the rotting pears left in our worked & heapt detritus will quicken the sap of one who'll seek to re-voice the sun.

astonished breath call

18.

a	s	w	s	a	s	j
	l	o	e	n	u	i
m	***o***	***r***	***n***	***i***	***n***	***g***
i	w	d	t	m	g	
d			i	a		e
d	g	***b***	***e***	***l***	***l***	***y***
e	i	e	n	i	i	e
n	f	q	t	k	g	\
	t	u		e	h	o
i		e	a		t	p
s	***t***	***a***	***r***	***t***	***l***	***e***
	o	t	t	e	y	n
h		h	f	x		
i	u	e	u	t	t	l
s	s	d	l	s	o	

morning belly startle

Koda *

lair slipt tongue
dream knit genitalia
swirling Aureole chapel
claw metal clasp
Lattice fluted grief
dormant fountain host
claspt unseen Palimpsest
Rimbaud wept silences
dangling Dream unspent
breath tongues Quarry
rose burnisht Wing
still undreamt stirring
Night's labial Dividends
another radiant Gutter
clasping parenthetical pulp
snow bloated roots
astonished breath Call
morning belly startle

* see p.120

The Koda, which was written first, is a selection of three words from each section of Roy Kiyooka's *the Fontainebleau Dream Machine: 18 Frames from A Book of Rhetoric.* Kiyooka has described his work, which consists of text & collages, as his "oftimes bemused Homage to the whole domain of European Art", of which, along with "Christianity & its twin, Capitalism", he saw himself "an errant child, an orphan". Kiyooka's second book of poetry, *Nevertheless These Eyes*, was a response to the life & works of Stanley Spencer, but he would move away from the early European influences.

I then wrote those words back into the haibun's prose sections as homage to one Nisei artist's life & workings through some of the vast grievances of that most grievous century, the Twentieth. It seems right to end such a tribute on a startle: he is an awakener.

Pacific Windows: Collected Poems of Roy K. Kiyooka, despite my misunderstanding in part 12, is still in print & available from Talon Books, Vancouver, BC, Canada for $24.95 [US]. As well as its value in gathering Kiyoooka's often fugitive texts, the book is remarkable in its fidelity to the original publications & illustrations.

Acknowledgements

the Writing offers much gratitude to many for phrasings, imagings, musics & stances that have seeded it. They're an unruly band of angels. Memory cannot be trusted to name all, but many of their traces show in the work. Especial thanks, however, are due to the late Fred Douglas & Roy Kiyooka and the present Deanna Ferguson for their adventures in the polis of art: the curiosity, the mirth, the pain & the swagger.

for episodic &/or sustaining encouragements the Author wishes to thank *Dave Simpson, Lyn Richards, Nate Dorward, Randolph Healy, Lissa Wolsak, Ted Byrne, the Kootenay School of Writing Collective circa 1998-2004, Kamloops Poets' Factory & Greenstone Mountain Collective, Kevin Nolan.*

for putting these works (a selection from the decade 1998 to 2008) into print, huge thanks go to:
Randolph Healy, *20/20 Vision* — Wild Honey Press, 1998;
Peter Riley, some poems from *One-Eye-Saw* appeared in *Harm's Length* – Poetical Histories #53, 2001;
Peter Philpott, *Evacuation Procedures*: *Great Works* (on-line) 2002'ish;
rob mclennan, *Strum of Unseen*: above/ground press (revised here), 2008;
Nate Dorward, *48 Out-takes from the Deanna Ferguson Show: Antiphonies*, The Gig (as *63 Out-takes from the D.F. Show* — revised here by further removals), 2008;
Kootenay School of Writing Collective, parts of *Evacuation Procedures & Mother Tongue Father Silence* first published in *W3*, 2000, & *W7*, 2003;
Susan Schultz, *MTFS* full version in *Tinfish* 14, 2004;
AND to Tony Frazer for his extraordinary enterprise, Shearsman, & for giving this work a home there

for keeping the planets around & bringing the sun up every morning – regardless of clouds etc – deep thanks Lyn Richards, wise mind & heart, my without-whom-knot.

www.ingramcontent.com/pod-product-compliance
Ingram Content Group UK Ltd.
Pitfield, Milton Keynes, MK11 3LW, UK
UKHW041937190726
13854UKWH00004B/1646

9 781848 614116